Preface

I created the Waste2Treasure entity and opened the site on September 23, 2023. Back then, we had our long URL: *sites.google.com/view/waste2treasure*, which later became just *www.waste2treasure.org* once we started our digital impact. At the day of writing this, January 20th of 2024, we're a fiscally sponsored organization working to change the world.

Thanks to all our donors, and HCB for fiscal sponsorship.

Oh, and a big thanks to you. Whether you're reading a sample, bought an eBook or doing it the wasteful way (print), this book will show you the way. (And, if you bought the print book, I'll leave it up to you to reduce the waste of this. Perhaps, gift it to someone when you're done reading?) **Every single penny earned from this book goes 100% to our causes**. While many nonprofits charge an administrative fee to make a profit, Waste2Treasure is completely dedicated to its cause, and we hope it'll always be.

-Ishan Bhat, Lead Of Waste2Treasure

Maya kicked at the pile of discarded clothes, a rainbow of forgotten fashion choices spilling from a burst bin. Plastic hangers lay scattered like bones on the asphalt, and a lone shoe, sole split and laces frayed, seemed to stare accusingly at the sky. This wasn't just any overflowing bin; it was the maw of the MegaMall, a behemoth of excess where trends were devoured and spat out faster than popcorn kernels.

Maya sighed. She wasn't some eco-warrior draped in hemp sandals and bedazzled kale, but this blatant waste gnawed at her. It wasn't the mountains of clothing that bothered her most, it was the stories they whispered – of impulse buys and fleeting desires, of resources swallowed and spat out like unwanted selfies.

That's when a flash of emerald caught her eye. Nestled amongst the polyester carnage was a vintage scarf, its silk whisper-thin and patterned with faded flowers. Maya picked it up, the fabric cool against her skin. In its frayed edges, she saw not decay, but potential. A story waiting to be rewritten.

With that, a spark ignited in Maya's chest. Maybe reducing waste wasn't about grand pronouncements and hair shirts. Maybe it was about finding the stories in the discarded, the beauty in the forgotten. Maybe it was about breathing new life into what others deemed worthless, stitching together a patchwork world where nothing was truly gone, just waiting to be reborn.

The next day, Maya returned to the MegaMall, not with a shopping bag, but with a toolbox. She wasn't there to buy, but to barter, to mend, to upcycle. Armed with needle and thread, a can of paint, and a head full of possibilities, she transformed cast-off treasures into whimsical creations. A chipped teacup became a planter, a dented bicycle helmet a funky chandelier, a stack of forgotten magazines a vibrant collage.

Word spread like wildfire. Soon, others joined Maya's crusade, their garages becoming workshops, their trash bins transformation stations. The MegaMall, once a monument to disposability, became a hub of reimagination, a canvas for a thousand second chances.

This is the story of the Waste2Treasure followers; not eco-warriors, but ordinary people who found magic in the mundane, beauty in the broken, and a whisper of hope in the echoes of waste. It's a story of rebellion, not against consumption, but against the idea that things are ever truly gone. It's a story about finding the extraordinary in the everyday, and stitching together a future where waste becomes not an ending, but a thrilling new beginning.

This is just the first page, the first stitch in a tapestry woven from discarded threads.

But that raises an important question; what specifically *can* we do?

The AI Community

Recently, I uploaded a new episode to my podcast. It was called "Reducing Waste Fast Facts" and came in 2 parts. Many people enjoyed that episode, so, the third part of that series will be in this book. Here we go with **Day 1**:

1. **Techie Tom, San Jose, California:** Upgrade your electronics smartly. Tom suggests investing in modular devices with upgradeable components to reduce electronic waste.
2. **Podcast Penny, Austin, Texas:** Host a virtual swap meet. Penny encourages podcast listeners to exchange items they no longer need, turning waste reduction into a social event.
3. **Vibrant Vicky, Miami, Florida:** Create art from recyclables. Vicky believes in turning waste into vibrant masterpieces, inspiring creativity while reducing trash.
4. **Silicon Valley Stan, Palo Alto, California:** Encourage your workplace to go paperless. Stan knows that embracing digital documentation can significantly reduce office waste.
5. **Eco-Fashion Fiona, Portland, Oregon:** Embrace sustainable fashion. Fiona suggests upcycling old clothes into trendy new outfits, proving that eco-friendly can also be stylish.

Day 2

1. **Innovative Ingrid, Seattle, Washington:** 3D print useful items. Ingrid recommends exploring 3D printing to create personalized, functional items and minimize waste.
2. **Gamer Greg, San Francisco, California:** Opt for digital downloads. Greg urges gamers to choose digital versions of games over physical copies, reducing plastic packaging.
3. **Clever Chef Charlie, New Orleans, Louisiana:** Get creative in the kitchen. Charlie proposes using food scraps to make homemade broths, reducing kitchen waste while enhancing flavors.
4. **Traveler Tessa, Honolulu, Hawaii:** Pack a zero-waste travel kit. Tessa advises travelers to bring reusable containers and utensils to minimize single-use items on the go.
5. **Virtual Vince, Raleigh, North Carolina:** Attend virtual events. Vince encourages attending online conferences and meetings to cut down on the environmental impact of travel.
6. **DIY Diane, Detroit, Michigan:** Make your cleaning supplies. Diane recommends DIY cleaning solutions using simple ingredients to reduce plastic packaging waste.
7. **Bike Commuter Benny, Salt Lake City, Utah:** Utilize a bike-powered phone charger. Benny suggests combining exercise with technology to power your devices sustainably.

Day 3

1. **Green Gamer Grace, Boston, Massachusetts:** Gamify your sustainability efforts. Grace proposes turning waste reduction into a game, rewarding yourself for eco-friendly habits.
2. **Coffee Connoisseur Carl, Charleston,** South Carolina: Invest in a coffee grinder. Carl suggests grinding your coffee beans to reduce packaging waste from pre-ground coffee.
3. **Green Gardener Gary, San Diego, California:** Create a compost tea for plants. Gary recommends using nutrient-rich compost tea as a natural fertilizer for your garden.
4. **Bookworm Bella, Madison, Wisconsin:** Utilize e-books and audiobooks. Bella advocates for digital reading options to reduce the environmental impact of paper production.
5. **Upcycling Uma, Asheville, North Carolina:** Transform glass jars into storage containers. Uma encourages turning empty jars into stylish and functional storage solutions.
6. **Mindful Marketer Mike, Minneapolis, Minnesota:** Embrace sustainable marketing materials. Mike suggests using eco-friendly promotional items to reduce marketing-related waste.
7. **Remote Worker Riley, Boulder, Colorado:** Opt for a reusable desk calendar. Riley recommends using a reusable whiteboard calendar to minimize paper waste.

Day 4

1. **Green Gift Greta, Burlington, Vermont:** Give experiences instead of physical gifts. Greta promotes gifting memories to reduce the environmental impact of material presents.
2. **DIY Dwayne, Anchorage, Alaska:** Create your beauty products. Dwayne encourages making skincare items at home using natural ingredients to reduce packaging waste.
3. **Adventure Alice, Phoenix, Arizona:** Pack a zero-waste hiking kit. Alice suggests bringing reusable utensils and containers on outdoor adventures to minimize environmental impact.
4. **Social Media Maven Sam, Savannah, Georgia:** Spread the word on social media. Sam encourages sharing waste reduction tips online to inspire others to join the movement.
5. **Green Grocer Giselle, Chicago, Illinois:** Choose produce with minimal packaging. Giselle advises selecting fruits and vegetables without excess plastic to reduce grocery waste.
6. **Mindful Musician Max, Las Vegas, Nevada:** Stream music responsibly. Max recommends using eco-friendly streaming services and supporting artists who prioritize sustainability.
7. **Tech Savvy Tanya, Santa Cruz, California:** Opt for repair over replacement. Tanya suggests learning basic device repair skills to extend the lifespan of your gadgets.

Day 5

1. **Artistic Andy, Portland, Maine:** Create recycled paper art. Andy encourages turning old newspapers and magazines into unique pieces of art.
2. **Eco Explorer Elijah, Denver, Colorado:** Use a reusable map. Elijah suggests investing in a durable, waterproof map for outdoor adventures instead of disposable paper maps.
3. **Gadget Geek Gina, Sacramento, California:** Donate old gadgets. Gina recommends giving outdated electronics to schools or organizations that can repurpose them.
4. **DIY Devin, Santa Fe, New Mexico:** Craft reusable cloth napkins. Devin encourages sewing your cloth napkins to reduce paper waste during meals.

Write Your Own Tips

If you're going to gift this book to someone (even yourself!), here's some space:

____

____

____

____

____

____

____

____

The Definition Of "Waste"

If someone asked me what 'waste' is, I could prove a technically-accurate complicated answer, like, *Waste, in the intricate tapestry of ecological discourse, constitutes the superfluous and residual detritus emanating from human consumptive endeavors,* or I could just say *"things we don't need."* Now, if someone asked me to talk about reducing waste... now that's hard to say. What if someone asked you to explain *gaming*? That's hard to define. Try defining the works *should, could, and would* without using any of those words in their own definitions. Defining "Waste" is complicated. If you're still reading, you're *using* your time wisely. But someone might still tell you that you're *wasting* your time.

How you want to define the terms "Reducing Waste" depends on how you think of the world. But, I promise, everything I share here will have some sort of direct or indirect impact on the environment, generally in a good way.

So, with that cleared, let's move on to some of the negative impacts of waste.

The Negative Impacts

Waste is bad. Common sense. I mean, figure out a way to make waste *good*, directly! What are the bad things? Too much to say. But a page should tell you enough.

- **Unclean Water.** Ever heard of the term "Microplastics" But guess what: there's microplastics in tap water. There's microplastics in some bottled water. And how much in microplastics do we consume by the end of the week? <u>As much as a credit card!</u> Can you believe it?
- **No Water.** Bad water is one thing. But, if we waste water too much, it'll only become less and less accessible. Already, the tons suffering without water, while we run it while we brush our teeth? That's not a good action plan. Your house could be next if you don't save water! (That's a little dramatic, but...)
- **No Planet.** We make waste. It goes in the garbage truck. And then it goes to a landfill, who knows where it is?
- **Inferior Quality Soil.** Everything depends on the Sun. Point is; you can trace almost anything back to organic material or metal (plastic might be the most foreign). Organic material grows in soil. Food grows in soil. No Soil = No Humans. So, without nutrients, soil is inferior in quality. <u>Bad Soil = Bad Humans!</u>

Why Reduce Waste?

In too many ways, reducing waste is not only good for you indirectly, reducing waste is *directly* good for you!

- **Environmental Benefit.** We all live in an ecosystem where everything depends on each other and is very interconnected. But, the moment one of these things break, we notice bad things. We keep abusing the very machine that we rely on. And, once this machine breaks, we cry. Everything around you came from the earth: you have to treat it well.
- **Economic Benefit.** Do you know how much money is wasted because we throw food away? (If you listen to our podcast, you'd know!) <u>The average family wastes $1500 in uneaten food every year!</u> I'd like to see you put $20 in the trash can (I mean, recycling bin)!
- **Social Benefit**. Usually, old sayings are good things. But the old saying "teamwork makes the dream work" sometimes falls apart. Point is; <u>you, yourself, can make a huge impact!</u> Reducing waste is a billion-person job but also a single person job. And, by looking at you, others will WANT to reduce waste. That's social impact. You don't have to do much. Just a little. Then the world changes right by your eyes. The entirety of this book was written by one person. So, printing double sided *does* make a change!

Now, all of that is at a very large scale. How will reducing waste help you at home? Well, here 'ya go!

- **Saving Money.** Remember how I just said about how you can save around $1500 in your family just by reducing uneaten food? That doesn't mean overeating; it means buying a little less, and finding out how much you TRULY need.
- **Living Healthier.** Back in the old days, there wasn't a thing called healthcare; because health didn't need care. Health was always there. Now, human health is only declining. But what wasn't there in the old days? WASTE. Reduce Waste = Increased Health. The "health" portion of reducing waste is generally complicated to explain; you'll understand it later in the book.

Pirates Say It Better.

Making A Difference. Arrr matey! Usually, ye ol' sayings be treasures worth cherishin', but the ancient wisdom of "teamwork makes the dream work" be a bit like a leaky ship in a storm. The point be, ye, yerself, can unleash a tidal wave of impact! The battle against waste be a quest fer a billion souls, but make no mistake, it be a quest for a single soul too.

Look at ye, settin' an example! Others will be drawn to the cause like sailors to the siren's song. That's the social impact, savvy? Ye don't need to haul the anchor all by yer lonesome. Just a wee bit effort from each soul, and behold, the world shifts right before yer eyes. This entire tome, a creation of one lone buccaneer.

Bought it in print, did ye? Well, that be a gold doubloon (~$1) cast into the treasure chest for our noble cause! And mind ye, there be more room in the chest for additional contributions, if ye catch me drift. Now, be that single doubloon enough to stem the tide of waste from this literary vessel? Nay, not by a long shot! But mark me words, I have faith in ye.

Will ye share this tome, or perhaps embark on a quest to pick up more litter, or even pledge allegiance to the sacred art of double-sided printing? Aye, that be the impact we seek! So, me heartie, go forth and make a mark on this vast sea of change! Yarrr!

Section 1
Rethink Your Habits

Transforming Waste2Treasure by Ishan Bhat

We Learnt It In School.

A long, long time ago, we all probably learnt about the classic "Reduce, Reuse, and Recycle" ideology which was pretty important... but none of us cared, or even though about the correct interpretation. Well, this ideology has evolved into not only **5 R's** but also a systematic hierarchy. With the addition of *Rethink* and *Refuse*, many principles in this hierarchy have changed. In fact, if you ask an AI what the 20 R's for the environment are, here's what you'll get:

1. **Reduce**
2. **Reuse**
3. **Refuse**
4. **Recycle**
5. **Repair**
6. **Rethink**
7. **Regenerate**
8. **Respect**
9. **Reforest**
10. **Replenish**
11. **Restore**
12. **Reskill**
13. **Renew**
14. **Reconnect**
15. **Reinvest**
16. **Responsibility**
17. **Reform**
18. **Reeducate**
19. **Reimagine**
20. **Reflect**

Who's Superior

So, now that we've gotten a look at how there are soooo many R's, we'll keep to our 5: **Reduce, Reuse, Recycle, Rethink,** and **Refuse.**

- <u>Refuse</u> is at the first place in this hierarchy, for obvious reasons. Because, if you say "no" to something, then it's impossible for you to have any waste coming from that thing.
- <u>Rethink</u> comes in next place, because, in this situation, you are almost going to buy something. At this time, we should think, *do I really need this or not.*
- <u>Reduce</u> is the third most important. Although both of the above are very good forms of reducing, the object of reducing is to ask ourselves *can I make do with a little less of this* in a sense that we're not overusing resources like water, shampoo, or sunlight. Ok, not the sunlight.
- <u>Reuse</u> is the second-to-last because if you come to the point where you have to reduce something, it means that you must have had some waste first. So, if everything above isn't possible or it's too late, well, this is the last chance before you're completely screwed.
- <u>Recycling</u> is the last: because it's *nearly* just as good as throwing something in the trash. Only around 6% of 'recycled' material actually gets recycled. In a perfect world, where knuckleheads wouldn't contaminate: recycling may have been practical!

PRACTICAL TIPS #1

Problem2Solution

Single-use items like plastic bags, water bottles, and coffee cups contribute significantly to plastic pollution.

Creative Fix: Embrace reusables! Carrying your own alternatives is a simple yet impactful way to reduce waste.

2Quotes

Waste not, want not—let's create a sustainable tomorrow by cherishing today's resources and sculpting a cleaner, greener legacy.

In the art of living, minimizing waste is the brushstroke that paints a canvas of ecological wisdom—a masterpiece of mindful choices echoing through the corridors of our planet's future.

A Letter From...

So, let's talk about some cool tricks to tackle everyday challenges. You know, those moments when you're tempted to buy that shiny toy or grab all the freebies in sight? Yep, we've all been there! Now, as your honorary President of Smart Choices, here are some super-duper creative solutions for these common challenges.

Resisting Impulse Purchases:

The 24-Hour Rule: When you see something you really, really want, wait for 24 hours before making the purchase. It's like giving your brain a chance to think it over. Sometimes, the excitement fades, and you realize you don't need it that much.

Budget Buddy: Have a friend or family member be your budget buddy. Before making any impulsive buys, give them a call. Talk it out! They might offer a fresh perspective that helps you make a smarter decision.

DIY Fun: Instead of buying something new, think about creating it yourself. Get crafty! You'll not only save money but also have a one-of-a-kind creation to show off.

Saying No to Freebies:

Purposeful Positivity: Politely say no with a smile. You can say, "No, thank you, I'm on a mission to declutter my life!" It's not about rejecting kindness but embracing a simpler, more intentional lifestyle.

Prioritize Needs: Before grabbing every freebie in sight, ask yourself if you really need it. If it doesn't serve a purpose or bring you joy, it might be better off staying right where it is.

Kind Sharing: Instead of taking everything for yourself, share the wealth! If you find freebies that you won't use, share them with friends, family, or even donate to a local charity. It's a win-win!

Remember, my young pals, making smart choices isn't just about saving money; it's about creating a life that aligns with your values and brings you happiness. So go out there, face those challenges with a grin, and make the choices that make you proud! You've got this! ✨

-Ishan Bhat, President Of Smart Choices At Waste2Treasure

Common Problems

The below solutions are long-term; something you can advocate for:

Problem: Excessive plastic waste

Solution: Implement and enforce strict regulations on single-use plastics, promote the use of biodegradable alternatives, and invest in recycling infrastructure to reduce the environmental impact of plastic waste.

Problem: Electronic waste (e-waste) accumulation

Solution: Encourage electronics manufacturers to design products with easier recyclability, implement e-waste collection programs, and promote consumer awareness on responsible electronic disposal methods.

Problem: Food waste in households and restaurants

Solution: Educate individuals and businesses on proper food storage, implement composting programs, and support initiatives that redistribute surplus food to those in need.

Problem: Pollution from industrial waste

Solution: Enforce stringent environmental standards for industries, incentivize the adoption of cleaner technologies, and invest in research for sustainable waste management practices.

The World Of Reusing

It's infinitely possible to reuse. If you come to think of it, if people could reuse at 100% efficiency, we wouldn't have to make anything else. Fix the same clothes. Research reusable diapers. Sort and melt plastic. But then, it all boils down to MONEY! Doing all this is EXPENSIVE so nobody really works hard to do it. (In fact, in reality, nonprofits are becoming businesses almost trying to make a profit at this point. Waste2Treasure is 100% to the cause. We don't use any donated money for personal needs.)

So, how does this information help us? Well, hopefully it convinces *you* to try and reuse at your own house. That is, once you've already reduced.

There's just too many opportunities to reduce, which we can only understand, if we have a dose of AI.

You
What are some creative ways to use an old cereal box so I can reduce waste (that's not too cringe)?

ChatGPT
How about turning that cereal box into a funky notebook or journal cover? Cut it to the desired size, decorate it with doodles or colorful paper, and bind some blank sheets inside. You'll have a unique and eco-friendly way to jot down your thoughts without being too cringe-worthy!

You
Um, won't I need some paper to cover the cereal ads anyways?

ChatGPT
Good point! How about embracing the cereal box design as part of the charm? You can use the box's colorful graphics and text as a quirky background for your notebook cover. It's like repurposing the box's personality into a conversation starter for your journal!

Ok, I'll be honest: that was terrible. In fact, it helps prove that AI, which has the entire internet of knowledge at it's robo-tips still acts crazy. Reusing things creatively is a human job. Not an AI's. Here are some interesting ideas my friend came up with:

- **Clothing Swaps** are a great way to get rid of your clothes without having to buy clothes. Assume the scenario that you accidentally buy a size 10 shoe (but your size is 9!) and your friend buys a size 9 instead of a 10. A swap would be useful here. But swaps are better done on old clothes which you probably won't need.
- **Upcycling** is a term which you'll find a lot if you look up "waste reduction." But what on earth is "upcycling"? Downcycling is the process in which things break down to the point where you can't use them anymore. *Up*cycling is the process where broken-down or unusable items are fixed/repaired so they can be easily used once again.
- **Refillable Containers** are one of the world's most simplest ways to reduce waste. If you think about it, a refillable container can save hundreds of plastic containers. In fact, a refillable container doesn't have to be a ceramic or glass container. Try using that plastic one again. Really, you can reduce the carbon footprint of something like a plastic container that simply; use it twice, divide by 2, use is 20 times, divide by 20. (And, if you use is over and over 50 times, the carbon footprint will be just 2g of carbon dioxide equivalent; watch our video on carbon footprints to learn more).

A Comedy Show

Me: *Tell me some jokes on reducing waste.*
W2T Fan: *Just listen to your own podcast episode.*
Me: *No, tell me some new jokes.*
Google Gemini Pro: *I can tell you some good ones.*
W2T Fan + Me: *We're not looking for AI jokes.*
Google Gemini Pro: *Here you go anyways...*

What did the eco-friendly superhero say to the villain who was polluting the environment?

"Prepare to face the consequences of your trash-talking!"

Why did the recycling bin get a promotion at work?

Because it was always doing its best to reduce, reuse, and recycle!

What did the compost bin say to the food scraps?

"I'm going to turn you into something beautiful, so don't be a waste!"

Why did the plastic bag get a time-out?

Because it was caught littering!

An Unrelated Topic

In the heart of a bustling city lived Maya, a teenager with a passion for creativity. She loved drawing, painting, and transforming everyday objects into art. But amidst her artistic endeavors, Maya noticed a growing pile of scraps and unwanted materials. Cardboard boxes, paint tubes, even bits of fabric – they all seemed destined for the trash.

One day, while browsing online, Maya stumbled upon Waste2Treasure, an organization dedicated to waste reduction. Intrigued, she clicked on their website and was met with a treasure trove of information. Articles explained the environmental impact of waste, while youtube videos showcased the importance of carbon footprints.

Inspired, Maya started small. She transformed an empty cereal box into a quirky pencil holder, using colorful paints and leftover fabric scraps for decoration. An old yogurt container became a handy paintbrush holder, adorned with mosaic patterns made from broken pieces of jewelry. Soon, her room was filled with unique creations, each one a testament to her newfound commitment to reducing waste.

As Maya delved deeper into Waste2Treasure's resources, she discovered more than just crafting tips. The organization offered educational videos, podcasts, and even workshops (not really) that explored the bigger picture of sustainability. Maya learned about composting, responsible consumption, and the importance of advocating for change.

Fueled by this newfound knowledge, Maya decided to share her passion with others. She organized a craft night at her local community center, teaching friends and neighbors how to turn trash into treasures. The event was a hit, filled with laughter, creativity, and a newfound appreciation for reducing waste.

From that day on, Maya became a Waste2Treasure champion. She spread the word about their mission, organized clean-up drives, and even convinced her school to implement composting bins. Her journey, sparked by a simple website, had blossomed into a movement, inspiring others to embrace a more sustainable lifestyle.

And so, Maya's story became a testament to the power of Waste2Treasure and the boundless creativity that can bloom when we choose to reuse, reduce, and rethink our relationship with waste.

That night, even though Waste2Treasure received no donations at all, the impact on the word was worth a million dollars; something Waste2Treasure wanted from the very, very beggining.

Recycling Right

Recycling. What's the first think you think of? *"Solutions to all our problems here!"* is what most of you said. You couldn't be further from the truth. In fact, those of you who even mentioned haven't listened to my podcast, for sure (99% of people reading this). In the podcast episode with my guest, we explain why: *"While recycling is important, it's just one piece of the puzzle. The waste hierarchy prioritizes reduce, reuse, and rethink (refuse) before recycling."*

It's a common misconception that everything you recycle is recycled (it's confusing in those words) meaning that only a limited portion is completely and truly re—cycled.

So... how much is recycled?

A half?
<u>No!!!</u>

A quarter?
<u>No!</u>

Come on, it's got to be more than a tenth, right?
<u>Nope.</u>

How much?
Only 6%

But Why So Less?

The title has it. There's got to be a reason.

You know that *one* guy who spoils it all for us. Who decided to bring weapons and hijak planes? He practically invented TSA 3000000000 minute airline security checks. However, most of the time, the case is that someone unknowingly ruins it for all. For example, recycling. Someone puts soiled containers. The mess spreads through tons of recyclable material and instantly converts it into garbage. *"Well, if those knuckleheads are contaminating our recycling anyways, then why should I care about not recycling."* A knucklehead asked that. If you've read the last 28 pages: you should know better than to ask that.

<u>Understand that, sometimes, it's better to throw something into the trash can than to throw a soiled version of it that could harm more perfectly good recyclable material!</u> If you're one of the more dedicated ones, use a little water (no wasting) to quickly rinse a soiled plastic container to recycle it.

 **ChatGPT**
Dear recyclers,

Throwing dirty containers into the recycling bin can harm the process. Rinse out food residue before recycling. Let's keep it clean together.

Thanks,
ChatGPT

Don't See A Bin, Pls!

I pray that these items never end up in a recycling bin, the same way a $100 note never sees one.

Visit A Bin ASAP Pls!

I pray that these items always end up in a recycling bin, <u>unlike</u> the way a $100 note never sees one.

The Treaty Of Rycle

It has come to the attention of the Waste2Treasure group that there have been several violations of concisely stated rules regarding the field of reducing waste. For this reason, the Treaty of Rycle has been formed in order to further clarify these laws as stated in section 408(m)9 of the Waste2Treasure universal behavioral recycling code.

Section 408(m)9

I) No person shall be given permission to recycle materials that in any way, shape, or form, may negatively interact with other materials en route to a recycling facility.

II) All humans under the Waste2Treasure admiration state of being [*see* section 307(i)2] will recycle immediately after use, if and only if, the material is categorized by the local government of residence that such material(s) are "recyclable."

They're Obvious...

1. Avoid single-use plastics.
2. Refuse unnecessary packaging.
3. Recycle properly to prevent contamination.
4. Say no to disposable products.
5. Minimize food waste by meal planning.
6. Use reusable items whenever possible.
7. Repair instead of replacing.
8. Opt for digital over paper whenever feasible.
9. Compost organic waste to reduce landfill impact.
10. Choose products with minimal packaging.

If you're not doing these 10 extremely obvious things already, it's time to re-read the educational text on waste2treasure.org! **Coming up is a basic test** on reducing waste, and to pass it, these are just some of the things that you need to start doing in order to pass!

Circle The Mistakes

Once upon a time in a not-so-distant land, there lived a remarkable individual named Wasteful Wendy. Now, Wasteful Wendy had a peculiar talent – she could turn even the simplest of tasks into a grand display of extravagance and waste.

One sunny morning, as the birds chirped and the flowers bloomed, Wendy decided it was the perfect day to embark on her mission to defy logic and common sense. With a skip in her step and a gleam in her eye, she set out to the grocery store.

As she strolled down the aisles, Wendy grabbed items with reckless abandon, tossing them into her cart with no regard for necessity or reason. "Who needs one loaf of bread when you can have ten?" she exclaimed, her voice echoing through the store.

Next, she made her way to the produce section, where she marveled at the vibrant array of fruits and vegetables. But instead of carefully selecting what she needed, Wendy grabbed handfuls of each, heedless of the fact that she could never consume it all before it rotted away.

With her cart overflowing with unnecessary purchases, Wendy made her way to the checkout counter, a triumphant smile plastered across her face. The cashier raised an eyebrow at the mountain of goods before him, but Wendy simply waved him off, insisting that she needed every last item.

Back at home, Wendy's wasteful ways continued unabated. She cooked elaborate meals for herself, using every pot, pan, and utensil in her kitchen, only to take a few bites before declaring herself full and tossing the rest in the trash.

But Wendy's wastefulness didn't stop there. Oh no, she was just getting started. She left the lights on in every room of her house, ran the water for hours on end, and drove her gas-guzzling car to the corner store just to buy a single candy bar.

Word of Wendy's wasteful antics spread far and wide, and soon she became the laughingstock of the town. People shook their heads in disbelief at her absurd behavior, wondering how someone could be so oblivious to the consequences of their actions.

But despite the ridicule and scorn heaped upon her, Wendy remained steadfast in her commitment to waste. After all, why bother conserving when you could have everything your heart desired at the push of a button?

If only...

Section 2
Expand Your Impact

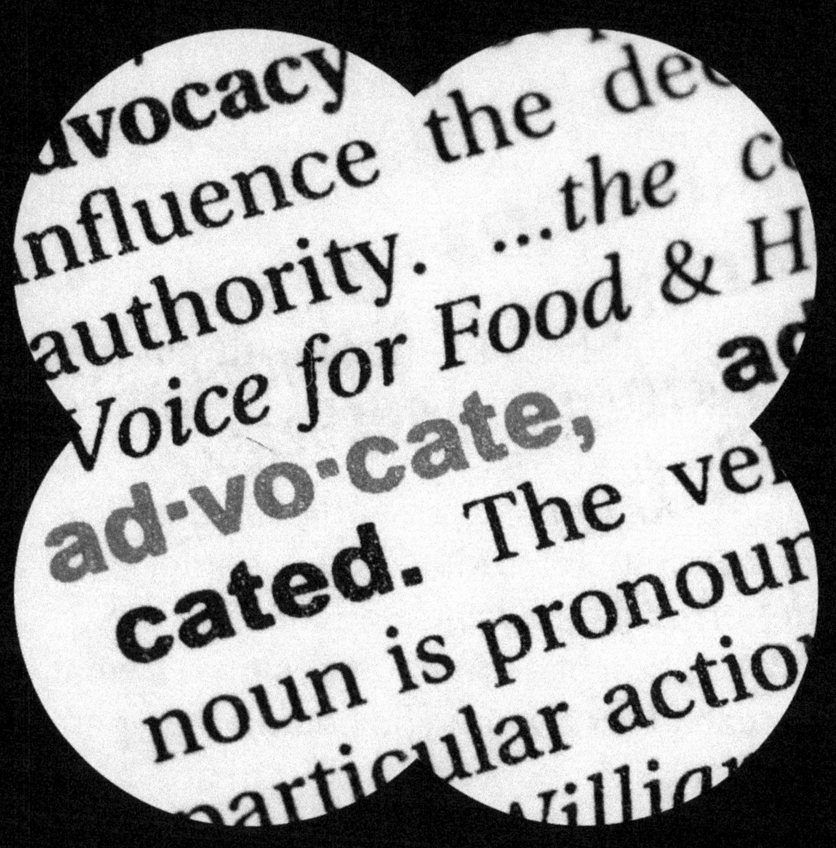

Advocating4Change

It's interesting that if you just want to See1Site you can visit Waste2Treasure which is all about Advocating4Change and Important8Types of Waste.

I started Waste2Treasure with just $12 back in september. Now, in mid-february as I write this, sometimes I wonder: how did my nonprofit become such a success; especially if you're reading this.

It's probably because I constantly advocated for the cause. I cared and still care so much about reducing waste that I've put in at least 50 hours of work so far; and it's gotten me here. Donations from various people, support from those around me, and the appreciation of acquaintances: that's what you can expect when you come around and do things like advocating. No, I'm not asking you to start a 501(c)3 and write a book. I'm not really asking you for a donation right now. I'm not even asking for your cooperation with my standards of waste-free living. I am asking for something so much more valuable than all of these things; I am asking for social impact, but maybe not in the way you think. I'm not asking you to tweet about this book. Definitely not asking you to send a copy of this book to all your friends.

I'm asking you to become your own 'organization'. Tell people about the importance of reducing waste. Educate the world about these things. Me alone? I'm doing lots. But I promise, you can do more. If it says on a piece of paper to "read this and hand it over to someone else that hasn't read it," the whole world will see that note. You and I are that note. We get people to read it, and we make sure they pass it on.

All this book, I've probably asked you to support Waste2Treasure, which is great. All I want you to know: you can do it too.

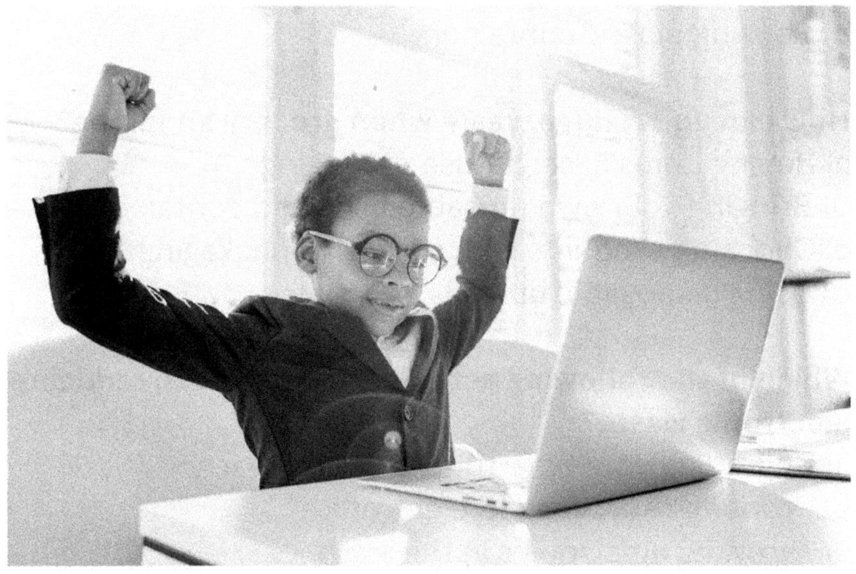

POP QUIZ!

What is the first step in reducing waste?
a) Recycling
b) Reusing
c) Reducing consumption
d) Composting

Which of the following items is NOT typically recyclable?
a) Glass bottles
b) Plastic bags
c) Aluminum cans
d) Cardboard boxes

What does the term "composting" mean?
a) Throwing away food waste
b) Breaking down organic matter into nutrient-rich soil
c) Recycling paper products
d) Reusing plastic containers

How can you reduce waste when grocery shopping?
a) Buying items in single-use packaging
b) Bringing your own reusable bags and containers
c) Choosing products with excessive packaging
d) Using disposable utensils and plates

Which of the following actions contributes to reducing electronic waste?
a) Upgrading your smartphone every year
b) Properly recycling old electronics
c) Throwing electronics in the trash
d) Keeping electronic devices turned on all the time

The Gallery

Here's some images that AI thinks represents the topic of reducing waste.

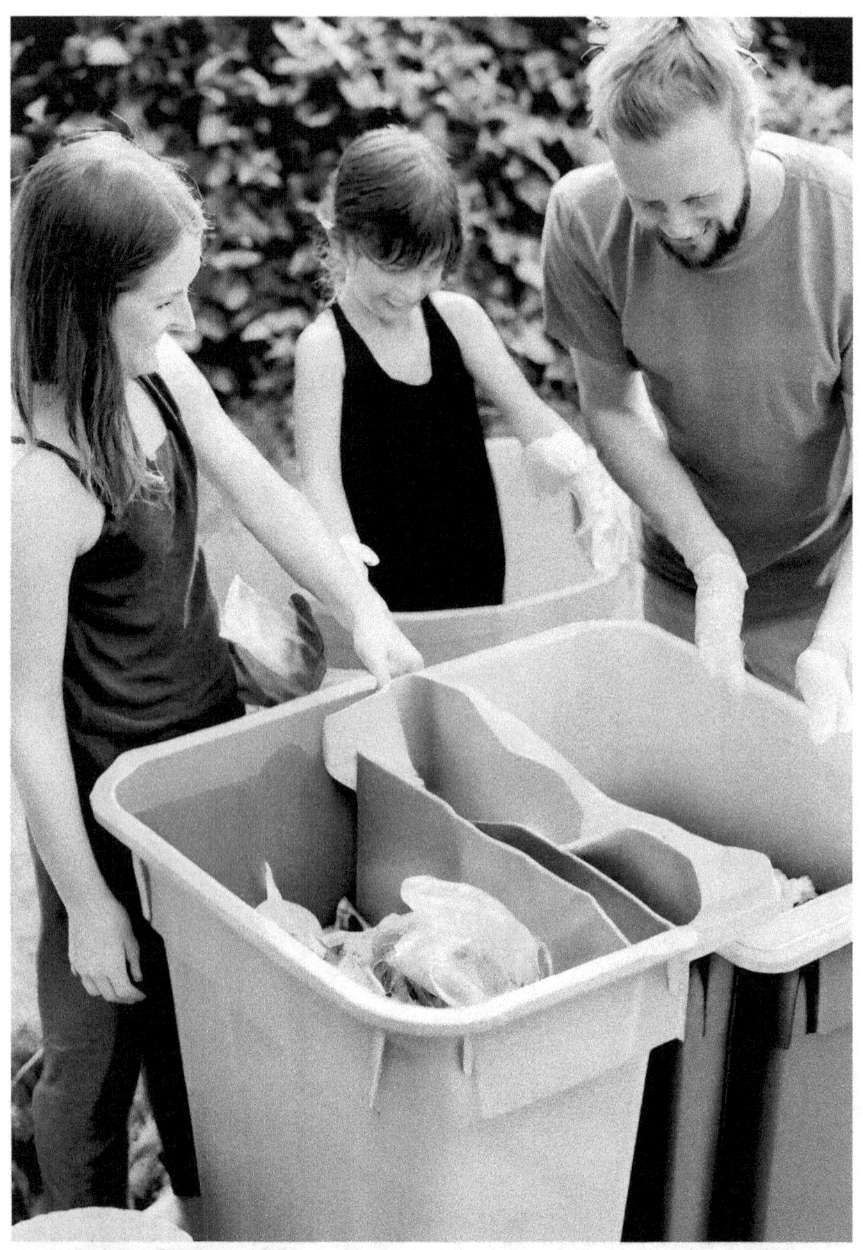

"A family sorting out their trash carefully and making sure that everything goes to the right bin."

"A large plot of on-roof land with growing boxes for plants in a bustling city."

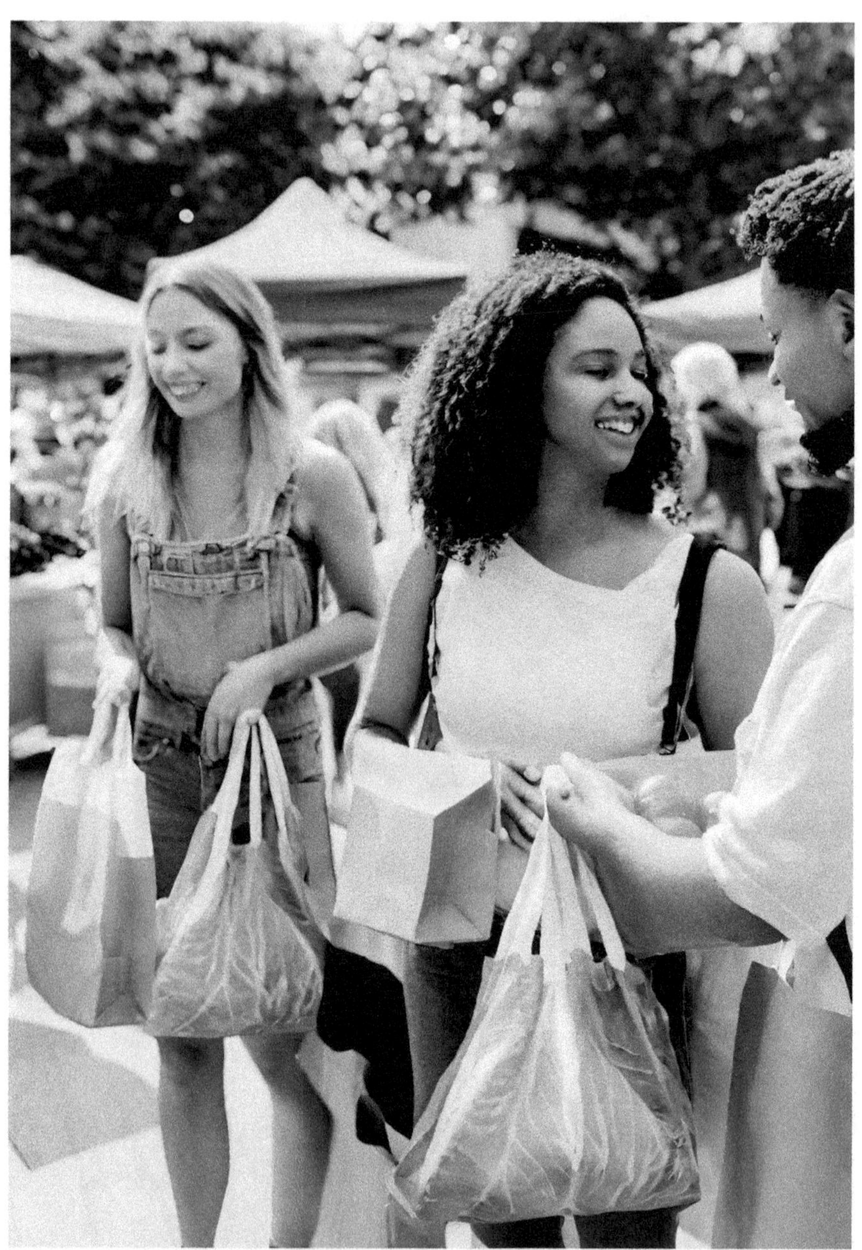

"A group of friends shopping at a local farmer's market, carrying reusable tote bags that look like vegetables."

"A group of people at a waste reduction workshop working busily to repair would-be trash into usable electronics by pooling their knowledge."

"A poster in a prominent city showing the impact of plastic on our ecosystems, while people look at it and understand the waste reduction ideology, if they don't know already! "

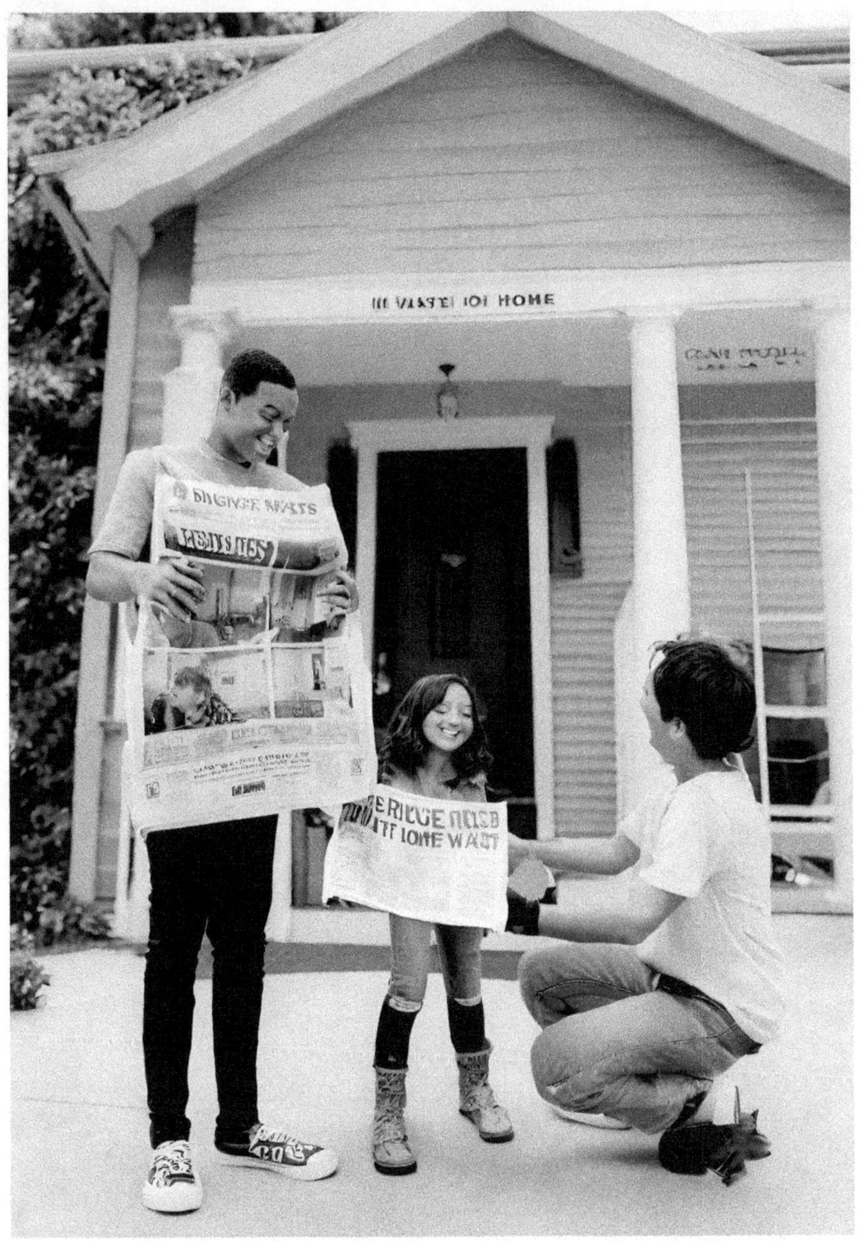

"A family holding up a detailed newspaper that has topics that relate to reducing waste at home, in front of a small suburban home."

"A massive city dedicated to maintaining the world's best eco-friendliness standards, with green building and plant-paved roads."

An informative sign, placed on a trailhead, explains the very important concept of reducing waste, and the sign itself is made out of natural wood, an impact-resistant board, and tree-free paper.

"A local teacher explains the very importance of reducing waste at a young age, and children in the classroom listen attentively to her."

A very eco-friendly car has a beautiful interior and exterior and looks a lot like a famous sports car, with large green wheels and minimalist design.

PRACTICAL TIPS #2

Problem2Solution

Food waste, which shouldn't exist, is occuring at a super-rapid rate. At the same time, rich soil full of nutrients is slowly dissapearing.

Creative Fix: Get a composter! Your food waste turns into rich soil, so you can grow plants in it! Win-Win-Win

3Quotes

Composting is nature's way of recycling, turning waste into nourishment for new growth.

In the dance of decomposition, composting teaches us the beauty of transformation and the harmony of returning to the earth what it has graciously provided.

Composting isn't just about scraps; it's a symphony of sustainability, orchestrating a greener future from the harmony of organic matter.

WHAT AN IDEA  !

Try Composting

Composting is like recycling food scraps and yard waste to make super-nutritious soil for your plants. It cuts down on trash, saves money on fertilizer, and helps the environment by reducing pollution. Plus, it makes your plants extra happy and healthy!

It's Your Turn

Whether you know it or not, this book is slowly coming to an end. Before I write my glorious closing, I want you to do a reflection on the next page. If you borrowed this from the library, you can do this on another piece of paper. Here are 3 questions to answer: **How much have you changed after reading this book? How much do you plan to change after reading this book? How will you advocate for the cause of reducing waste?**

Closing

When I started writing this book, sometime in mid-december, I didn't have any intention to publish it formally. I didn't know my organization would be tax-exempt such that I could collect donations from my 2 supporters; my parents. Today, Waste2Treasure is small but large. I don't know how much impact I made by writing all of this. I don't know how much impact I made by spending hours and days writing this book. But I always knew, everything started off small. Today's president *was* once a baby. When I shared the website, initially, on an AoPS forum, someone wrote to me "You may have great content, but your reach is too small." or something along those words. I wasn't demotivated, but another person posted on that same thread *"If you have to walk a mile, do not wait a year. Put one step after another and move forward."* And I think that's some great advice for you and I.

A book written by **Waste2Treasure Organization**'s founder, Ishan Bhat.

Visit

www.waste2treasure.org

Visit donate.waste2treasure.org for tax-exempt options.

Exclusive Edition

Since you purchased the exclusive version of this book, you get some Waste2Treasure perks.

1. Free eBook For Friend
2. Free eBook(s) For Future W2T Books
3. Free Access To Exclusive Online Content (Coming Soon)
4. Talk To Our Team (About Anything)
5. More Perks On Future *Things* We Do; Visit **exclusive.waste2treasure.org** to see more things or even *request* something from us!
6. Bragging Rights
7. The Proudness

To access these perks, you must have the paperback version of this book. Make a SHORT video of flipping through the last 3-4 pages, including this one. Then, email it to team@waste2treasure.org. Since these perks aren't 100% guarenteed, this exclusive edition is sold at the same price as the standard. It's a game of who can find it!